AF270512

BIRDS

BY A. W. BUCKEY

Essential Library

An Imprint of Abdo Publishing
abdobooks.com

Cover Photo: Eric Isselee/Shutterstock Images
Interior Photos: Eric Isselee/Shutterstock Images, 1, 97; Murilo Mazzo/Shutterstock Images, 3, 88–89; Shutterstock Images, 4–5, 12, 21, 24 (bottom), 44, 52, 60, 101; Animaflora PicsStock/Shutterstock Images, 7; iStockphoto, 11, 70, 76–77; Jiri Hrebicek/Shutterstock Images, 16; Nick Beer/Shutterstock Images, 18; Marvin Minder/Shutterstock Images, 20; Albert Art/Shutterstock Images, 24 (top); Tracy Starr/Shutterstock Images, 26–27, 100; Artem Tkachuk/Shutterstock Images, 29; Fillipe Brum/Shutterstock Images, 33; Aleksandar Blanusa/Shutterstock Images, 34; Juniors Bildarchiv/SuperStock, 36; Rosa Jay/Shutterstock Images, 40; Jill Lang/Shutterstock Images, 46; Igor Avramchuk/Shutterstock Images, 49; Andry Denisah/AFP/Getty Images, 50; Betty LaRue/Alamy, 55; James D. Morgan/Getty Images News/Getty Images, 62; Mamunur Rashid/NurPhoto/Getty Images, 64; Michelle McLoughiln/AP Images, 68; Romeo Gacad/AFP/Getty Images, 71; Patrick Semansky/AP Images, 75; FLPA/Alamy, 78; David Degner/Getty Images News/Getty Images, 81; Dan Wagner/Sarasota Herald-Tribune/AP Images, 83; John Daniels/Mary Evans Picture Library/SuperStock, 87; Rick Friedman/Corbis Historical/Getty Images, 90; VH-Studio/Shutterstock Images, 99

Editor: Marie Pearson
Series Designer: Becky Daum

Library of Congress Control Number: 2022948870

PUBLISHER'S CATALOGING-IN-PUBLICATION DATA

Names: Buckey, A. W., author.
Title: Birds / by A. W. Buckey
Description: Minneapolis, Minnesota: Abdo Publishing Company, 2024 | Series: Essential pets | Includes online resources and index.
Identifiers: ISBN 9781098290511 (lib. bdg.) | ISBN 9781098276690 (ebook)
Subjects: LCSH: Pets--Juvenile literature. | Cage birds--Juvenile literature. | Birds--Juvenile literature. | Pets--Behavior--Juvenile literature. | Zoology--Juvenile literature.
Classification: DDC 636.0887--dc23

CONTENTS

FRIDAY FLYDAY

It's the end of the school week, but Waseet doesn't have time for a break. He heads straight home from his last class and opens the door. As soon as Waseet gets inside the house, the sound of happy chirping fills the bottom floor. Waseet takes off his shoes and follows the noise to a large cage near his bedroom window. There, two small birds are flitting from their perches to the bars of the cage itself, yelling cheerfully for Waseet's attention. They're talking to him, and he's happy to talk back.

"Hi, Nickel. Hi, Dollar," Waseet greets the birds. "Happy Friday Flyday!"

Waseet opens the cage, and two small, friendly birds waddle toward his hand. Nickel and Dollar are members of a parrot species called the budgerigar (BUH-juh-ree-gahr). Usually called parakeets in the United States, these small, often brightly colored

Budgerigars have a wingspan of 10 to 14 inches (25–36 cm).

BUDGERIGARS IN NATURE

birds have curved beaks and long, elegant tails.

Waseet's birds are both about seven inches (18 cm) long.[1] They weigh slightly more than one ounce (28 g).[2] Nickel is mostly gray with a light blue belly, and Dollar is a bright green. Budgerigars are often called budgies, and Waseet's two birds have nicknames too: he's called them Nicky and Dolly ever since they were young. Dolly walks onto Waseet's wrist, and Nicky stays perched on his finger. He gives them both a quick pet on the head and then gently puts them on the perch by his study desk. They'll wait in his room while he gets everything ready.

Waseet goes to the kitchen and gets a small stalk of spray millet, a seed his birds love. It's like ice cream to them, so Waseet uses it as a treat and a motivation tool. When he needs his birds to pay attention, having the spray millet handy always helps. Before he opens the door to his bedroom, Waseet checks the house to make sure outlets are covered, the toilet seat is down, and no hazardous materials are lying around. He wants to be sure that Nicky and Dolly don't fly into danger.

TO THE AVIARY

When everything is ready, Waseet tucks the spray millet into his pocket and walks back to his room. Nicky and Dolly hop eagerly onto his hand and travel with him toward the backyard. There, Waseet has set up an aviary. This large, outdoor cage is about the size of a small car,

Aviaries can be homemade or purchased, but both kinds should be sturdy, and birds should not be able to escape from them.

giving the birds plenty of room to stretch their wings and fly around. Budgerigars are native to Australia and comfortable in warm weather, so this sunny April day in North Carolina is perfect for them.

Waseet is busy with school and sports during the week, and he doesn't always have time to give his birds outdoor exercise. Some days, they have to settle for supervised play in his room instead. But whenever the weather allows it, Waseet makes it home for Friday Flyday. Nicky and Dolly flutter joyfully around the aviary, stopping every now and then to play with their bell and rope toys. Waseet keeps an eye out, making sure they're secure in the cage. He loves watching them have fun.

THE DAILY ROUTINE

Waseet helps Dolly and Nicky follow the rhythms of the sun, as they might if they were in the wild. When the sky starts to darken a little, he uses spray millet and his voice to call Nicky and Dolly over to his finger. Waseet closes the aviary and brings his birds indoors, gently holding one in each hand. Once the birds are safely inside their indoor cage, Waseet starts to make them dinner. They'll get a seed mix from the pet store, along with a few fresh fruits and veggies that Waseet has prepared himself. He follows the recipe of his favorite online bird expert, and Nicky and Dolly eat it enthusiastically.

As usual, the budgies make a mess during dinner, getting seeds all over the bottom of the cage. Waseet sighs a little at the mess on the strips of newspaper, but he's happy his pets are enjoying their meal. Tonight, he'll just change the paper at the bottom of the cage. Tomorrow will be the weekly deep clean. After dinner, he talks with chatty Dolly and practices a new trick with Nicky. She's learning how to walk inside a toilet paper roll. Soon enough, Waseet knows, she'll master the trick, and then Dolly will be interested in trying it out too.

Waseet's parents will be home soon, and they will eat a human dinner and enjoy their evening. By then, Nickel and Dollar will be settled in

BIRDBATHS

In nature, birds bathe regularly in water sources they find. Water helps them rinse off their feathers, and they clean further by preening, or taking oil from a gland near the tail and spreading it over their feathers. Pet budgies need to bathe in lukewarm water using a shower, a sink, or a dish of water set aside just for them.

the quiet of his bedroom, ready for a full night's sleep and whatever adventures the weekend brings.

ANCIENT COMPANIONS, NEW CHALLENGES

The budgerigars who talk and fly in American homes are just one of the pet bird species that humans have loved for thousands of years. Today, about five million homes in the United States have a pet bird.[4] Bird owners are often surprised and delighted by their pets' intelligence and sociability and by the strong bonds they forge with their animals.

However, despite their often small size, birds can be loud, messy, and time-consuming pets. They are often surrendered to shelters by people who were not prepared for their care. Some people believe birds do not belong in the home at all. The pet bird industry is a complex global trade, but there are environmental and ethical concerns with the sourcing and raising of pet birds. Birds are diverse and demanding animals, not easily understood or cared for. But the people who do take on the challenge of responsible bird ownership often find it immensely rewarding.

Birds and their owners can form close bonds.

CHAPTER 2

THE HISTORY OF PET BIRDS

There are more than 11,000 known species of birds in the world.[1] Not all of them can or should be pets. It is difficult to imagine a household that could accommodate a penguin or an ostrich. However, a variety of birds have lived as pets at one time or another across thousands of years. There is a word for *birdcage* in Sumerian, a language dating to around 3000 BCE that is one of the oldest written languages in the world. One of the first domestic bird species was the pigeon. The pigeons of today's cities are descended from a species that was tamed by humans more than 6,000 years ago.

Over time, people realized that birds made intelligent, teachable companions and that songbirds could bring music and color to a home. In medieval Europe (500–1500 CE), it was

Some people enjoy racing their pigeons. The length of a pigeon race can be anywhere from 100 to 600 miles (161–966 km).

popular for royal women to keep local bird species in cages as pets. Later, European sailors brought back tropical birds from their travels, and birds such as the canary from Africa became trendy pets. Before the early 1900s, many Americans kept native North American bird species as pets. However, a law passed in 1918 made it illegal to keep most migratory, or traveling, North American birds as pets. Lawmakers were trying to prevent overharvesting of these birds. As a result, most pet birds are of species native to tropical regions, not to the United States.

DOMESTIC AND FERAL PIGEONS

Some of the first birds to be domesticated were pigeons. The ancient Greeks were among the early people keeping pigeons as pets. The pigeons that live in towns and cities today are descended from rock doves that were caught and bred by ancient people. These birds were first raised for their meat. Because pigeons have an excellent sense of direction and an ability to navigate using Earth's magnetic field, they were later used to carry messages.

Tropical birds have been traded and kept as pets for hundreds of years, so many of the birds used as pets today were born and bred in the countries from which they were sold. However, these birds still share the nature of their wild counterparts. They tend to prefer warm weather and a lot of sunlight, though their cages should not be placed right in front of a window, where animals outside could startle them.

There are about 7.5 million pet birds in the United States today.[2] These birds belong to many different species, and it is unknown exactly how many birds of each species live as American pets. In general, however, pet birds belong to two major groups: parrots and finches.

PET PARROT SPECIES

The word *parrot* is a general term for a bird from the order Psittaciformes, which includes about 360 species of bird.[3] This order includes budgerigars, cockatoos, cockatiels, macaws, parakeets, lovebirds, conures, lorikeets, and birds whose names have the word *parrot* in them. These birds vary greatly in size, appearance, and habitat, but they have several key features in common. Parrots tend to live in tropical to southern temperate regions in Asia, Oceania, Africa, and South and Central America. There used to be a native North American parrot called the Carolina parakeet. It lived in flocks and could be found as far north as Wisconsin. After losing its habitat to deforestation and suffering population loss due to hunting, the bird went extinct in the early 1900s.

Parrots range from four to 40 inches (10–102 cm) long.[4] They are social birds, living in groups or flocks, and most eat a diet based on vegetables, seeds, or fruit. Parrots have

hard, hooked beaks and muscular tongues. They are known for their intelligence and their ability to mimic, or imitate, the sounds they hear around them. This talent for mimicry is how parrots got the reputation for being able to talk. Many parrots can learn and repeat sounds they hear, sometimes including words and phrases.

A parrot's talking ability is not the same as a human's. The bird's vocal organs work much differently to produce the sounds it makes. In the wild, parrots make sounds to communicate with other birds, such as their parents and members of their flock. For example, wild parrots contact call, or use a call-and-response method to locate their loved ones. Pet parrots talk to fulfill this need to

Many species of parrots live in flocks. The red-and-green macaw usually lives in pairs but sometimes forms small groups.

be in touch with their caretakers. It used to be widely believed that although parrots could memorize sounds, they had no understanding of what they were saying. However, recent research has helped show that this is not necessarily the case.

A would-be parrot owner must consider many factors when deciding on a bird to bring home. Each type of parrot has its own unique and delightful traits, as well as some attributes, such as noisiness or a tendency to bite, that might make it a bad fit for a particular home. The budgie may be the most popular pet parrot species due to its small size and friendly nature. Another popular pet parrot is the cockatiel, a native Australian bird with a crest

Cockatiels grow up to 12 inches (30 cm) long, making them one of the smaller parrot species.

on its head. These two birds are sometimes considered good beginner parrots because they can introduce a first-time bird owner to the unique challenges of caring for birds, and they are not as high-maintenance as other species.

Many other parrot species live as pets too. The caique, a type of South American parrot, is known for its energy and eagerness to do tricks, but it can be quick to nip people. Larger parrots such as the Amazon are known for their messy ways and need for attention. For example, Amazon parrots love to splash water whenever they bathe and scatter food as they eat. These large parrots also have a lot of intelligence to go with their big personalities.

Cockatoos are long-lived and very sensitive, with the capacity to be affectionate as well as emotional. The galah, a cockatoo with a pink chest and head, is one of the most striking cockatoos and is in high demand. Conures, smaller South and Central American parrots known for their beauty, are also quite noisy. Lorikeets and lories are unique among parrots in that they eat a mostly liquid nectar diet.

PET FINCHES

Finches belong to the songbird suborder of the Passeriform order. Finches are found on every continent except Antarctica. They are small songbirds with

The lorikeet has a special tongue with what looks like a brush at the end that helps it get nectar from flowers.

cone-shaped bills. They tend to eat seeds in the wild. Birds use an organ called a syrinx to make sounds. In songbirds, this organ is very complex. It allows them to make elaborate songs and even sing two different notes at once.

Commonly known birds such as the sparrow are finches, but the most famous pet finch might be the canary. These brightly colored birds are native to islands off the west coast of Africa, including the Canary Islands, which gave the birds their name. Canaries have been kept as pets for hundreds of years, and breeders have selected the birds for bright colors and singing ability. Canaries in the wild are a blend of brown,

ZEBRA FINCH

While canaries are probably the best-known pet songbirds, the zebra finch has a reputation for being interesting and easy to care for. Zebra finches are native to Oceania, where they live in dry grasslands. They are named after the black-and-white stripes across their chests.

Zebra finches are small birds, measuring just 3.9 to 4.7 inches (10–12 cm).[5] Zebra finches mature quickly and are ready to begin breeding by six months old.[6] They mate easily and often, and zebra finch owners should be careful to make sure their birds do not exhaust themselves laying eggs and raising young.

In the wild, zebra finches bond with one mate for life. While these birds enjoy the company of other finches, they are not especially inclined to seek out human company. They may hop on a human hand, but they will not want to cuddle and play the way a parrot might.

They do, however, enjoy noises such as music on the radio or human speech. Zebra finches use sounds like chirps and trills to communicate with each other and express emotions. They can also memorize and vocalize complex melodies.

green, and yellow, but people can buy pet canaries in a variety of colors, including the popular bright yellow. Canaries, and finches in general, do not seek out human contact the way pet parrots do. They can be trained to sit on a human finger, however.

Canaries are probably best loved for their singing ability. Male canaries tend to sing more than the females do, although both sexes vocalize. Research into canaries has found that the birds have excellent memories for sounds and melodies. As young birds, canaries learn syllables, or blocks of melodies, that they memorize and reorganize into five- to 15-second songs. A canary can have up to 35 syllables in its vocal repertoire.[7] Other pet finch species include the zebra finch and the Gouldian finch, both native to Australia.

DOMESTIC BIRDS

Some domestic birds have lived alongside humans for thousands of years, but not as pets. Domestic animals are the descendants of wild animals that lived near or alongside humans. Over time, these animals were bred to make them adaptable to human purposes. For example, the domestic chicken's ancestors were the wild jungle fowl that lived in India. Eventually, the chickens raised, bred, and slaughtered by humans came to look and act differently than those wild birds. Domestic chickens, for example, are bigger and heavier than their jungle fowl ancestors, and they lay bigger eggs.

Other domestic birds include some types of ducks, geese, turkeys, quail, pigeons, and doves. Emus, while not domesticated over thousands of years as chickens were, are also sometimes raised for their meat and leather. When domestic birds are raised solely for their meat and eggs, they are not considered pets. However, there are some people who choose to keep these animals only as pets instead of for their typical purposes.

For example, in the United States, some people choose to keep chickens as pets. Chickens are flock animals, and they like to pick for seeds and insects outdoors. They are happiest in backyard or outdoor environments among other chickens of their flock. Pet chickens are typically housed in outdoor coops

CANARIES AND HUMANS

Spanish sailors found canaries on islands off the coast of Africa and brought them to Europe. After the 1500s, canaries became popular pets on the European continent. Canaries were also used to detect harmful gases in environments such as underground mines. The birds use a lot of oxygen and become ill from toxic air more quickly than humans do. The phrase "canary in the coal mine" for an early warning of trouble comes from this historic use of canaries. They have also made their way into popular culture: Tweety, a famous *Looney Tunes* character, is a canary.

for shelter and provided with a run, or a place to explore and exercise outside.

The line between pet ownership and domestication can be blurry in the chicken's case. For example, people who raise pet chickens may still collect and eat their pets' eggs, although they may not slaughter the birds for meat. However, some people do raise their chickens from a young age to be cuddly and loyal pets. They can learn to perform tricks and bond with their handlers. In addition, some chickens are bred to have beautiful or unusual physical features, such as fluffy plumes of feathers. Some people raise and train breeds of chickens to compete in poultry shows.

Some domestic roosters, *top,* still look similar to their wild male jungle fowl counterparts, *bottom.*

CHAPTER 3

PET BIRD CARE

Pet birds are small yet complex animals. While they do not require a great deal of food or water, they thrive in environments where their owners understand their unique needs and provide them with a safe and satisfying home. Wild parrots forage for food in flocks, eating the seeds, fruits, nuts, and sometimes insects native to their habitats. In captivity, most parrots do not need to eat the same seeds or plants they would have eaten in their native country. Parrots do well eating a variety of plants and seeds, even those from other regions.

However, feeding a parrot can be challenging because there are many parrot species and not a great deal of research into each of their nutritional needs. Therefore, feeding a pet parrot of any kind requires research as well as trial and error. Parrots in general have very high metabolisms and eat about one-fifth of their body weight in food daily.[1]

Nuts are part of many parrots' natural diets. Eating hard nuts helps file down their beaks, which grow continuously.

But the amount of food a parrot eats should be further adjusted to each bird's specific metabolism. Parrots in the wild get a lot more exercise than pet parrots, who are prone to becoming overweight and obese. Owners should monitor their birds' food intake and make sure they do not give them too many fatty foods and treats.

Birds like routines, and they appreciate being fed at set times. Many parrot experts recommend feeding birds two times a day, first thing in the morning and again in the evening. These early-morning and evening feeding times mimic a wild bird's foraging schedule. Parrot experts recommend that owners try to imitate the species' diet in the wild as best they can with ingredients locally available to them. One of the most important things to consider is variety. Parrots need a lot of different foods to stay healthy.

The basic ingredients of a pet parrot diet are vegetables, pellets, seeds, and treats. Parrots can eat many vegetables and fruits, including carrots, peppers, bananas, and oranges. They are capable of digesting whole grains such as beans and pasta too. Parrots can also be fed pellets, which are compacted food mixes designed to provide necessary vitamins and nutrients. Including a pellet blend in a parrot's daily diet helps guard against vitamin deficiencies or problems caused by poor nutrition. Parrots love nuts and seeds, but birds may eat too many

of them if they are always made available. Parrot experts recommend that nuts and seeds be available to birds in small amounts. Particularly tasty seeds can be reserved as treats or training rewards. For example, bird trainers sometimes use spray millet to help birds get more comfortable with human contact and company. If the spray millet is given too frequently, however, it loses some of its effectiveness as a special treat.

In addition, pet birds may sometimes need additional sources of calcium. Many bird experts recommend putting a cuttlebone inside a pet parrot's cage. Cuttlebones are the internal shells of cuttlefish, animals that resemble squids. Parrots can play with the cuttlebone by biting at it with their beaks, helping to smooth and

HUMAN FOOD FOR BIRDS

In addition to their regular diets, pet birds are allowed to eat some human foods. Feeding birds human food can be a way to bond with them and share the dining experience. There are some human foods that should always be off-limits to birds, however. Sugary, salty, and processed foods are not good for birds. Other commonly consumed foods such as chocolate, avocado, and alliums like onions are toxic to birds.

groom the beak as they do so. In the process, the cuttlebone can provide the bird with necessary calcium.

Pet finches, like parrots, eat seeds in the wild. They also love seeds like millet and may overeat or choose an unbalanced diet if left to eat seeds only. To avoid nutritional problems that can lead to poor health, veterinarians recommend that finches be fed specially formulated pellets alongside fresh fruits and vegetables and a small amount of seeds.

CAGES AND AVIARIES

A pet bird's cage is its home for most of its life, and it must be a safe and comfortable environment. Even birds who leave their cages for hours every day need an adequately sized cage. Three main considerations for a birdcage are size, materials, and the cage's placement in the home. Birds of different sizes will need different-sized cages. A minimum width that some bird experts suggest is two times the length of the bird's wingspan.[2] Others say three times the wingspan's length, but as a general rule, the bigger the cage, the better. The cage should also be tall enough to give the bird space: three times the bird's length or more is a good rule of thumb. If two birds are kept in the same cage, owners should follow the size guidelines for the larger of the two birds, and if three or more birds are kept together, the cage size should increase for each additional bird.[3]

A birdcage must be big enough for the bird to fly around, exercise, explore, and hide, in addition to having space for its food, water, toys, and perches. Perches are places for the bird to rest on inside the cage. These should be located so that the bird can stand on them without brushing the edge of the cage, and so that the birds can fly in a straight line from one to another. According to the Australian RSPCA, a leading animal welfare organization, "The minimum length of a cage should permit at least two wing beats (the more the better) between perches."[4] A good perch has an irregular shape, the way a natural tree branch does, in order to let the bird find its favorite type of footing. In fact, natural tree branches make great perches. Perches can be made out of artificial material as well, but they should not be coated with sandpaper or any other rough material that might damage a bird's feet. They should also not be slippery, like smooth plastic.

Pet bird owners should also pay close attention to the width of a cage's bars. Too narrow, and the bird will not be able to climb. Too wide, and the bird also cannot climb and may be able to escape. A good cage has both horizontal and vertical bars so that the bird can climb around easily. The best birdcages are made out of steel, which is too strong for parrots to break with their beaks. This steel can be powder coated, which is a method of painting the steel and then baking it to preserve and decorate it, but it should never be covered in plastic or vinyl. Birds can wear away at these coverings and end up accidentally eating them. Birdcages for parrots should be placed in well-lit, busy areas of the house. These social birds want the interaction that comes from people passing by their cages. However, pet birds should not be kept in the kitchen; there are too many hazardous materials and smells there.

It's important that a pet bird always has access to fresh, clean water. Birds bathe regularly by dipping in water or dew and spreading oil from a gland across their feathers. Ideally, a bird's bathing water and drinking water should be separate. Changing the bird's water cup

at each meal helps ensure that it always has fresh water ready to use. In addition to water, some parrots require humidifiers. Their skin can become very unhealthy in cold, dry environments, and the room they are caged in needs extra moisture to make the birds comfortable.

Birds eat, eliminate waste, drink, and bathe inside their cages. None of these processes are particularly clean. A birdcage should be cleaned daily so that poop and spilled food do not build up and cause a health hazard. Veterinarians recommend using newspaper or paper

Bathing helps keep a bird's skin and feathers healthy.

towels to line a bird's cage and changing out the lining every day. While commercial bird litter is available, it could be a health risk to birds if chewed or inhaled. Chewing paper, on the other hand, will not harm birds.

Birds also benefit from safely spending time outdoors. Aviaries are large outdoor cages designed to give pet birds space to fly. Many are homemade. In general, a good aviary is covered with mesh to prevent rodents and pests from getting in. It's well ventilated, giving birds fresh air. And a well-constructed aviary has many of the same features as a good cage, like perches and cups for fresh water.

BIRD PROOFING A HOME

Birds are small, mobile, and airborne. Pet bird owners should assume that a pet bird can and will access any

GALLIZZI

part of a home that is not actively closed off. This means that every room a pet bird can possibly access should be bird proofed.

The first step to bird proofing a home is making sure that birds cannot escape. Windows and doors to the outside should always be closed when a bird leaves its cage. Even clipped birds, or those whose wing feathers have been trimmed to reduce flight ability, may fly well enough to escape through a window. Bird proofing also involves removing any toxins or dangers from the bird's range of access. Birds have small lungs and can be easily overwhelmed by toxic fumes. They should never be exposed to smoke or spray cleaners and disinfectants.

In addition, pet bird owners should avoid buying kitchenware coated with Teflon, as it releases fumes toxic to birds when heated. They should make sure that birds are unable to access and chew physical hazards such as electrical wires. Pet bird owners should also be cautious about letting pets such as cats and dogs around birds. While some mammals can live peacefully with birds, predators such as cats have an innate instinct

Because many parrots' beaks and jaws were made to crack open hard nuts, it's important to keep valued belongings in a different part of the home than where a parrot is allowed free.

to hunt moving creatures. These animals can coexist only with close supervision. They should never be left alone together.

COMMON HEALTH AND SAFETY ISSUES

Birds' bodies are very different from the human body, and there can be a learning curve to understanding how a healthy bird looks and acts. In addition, most pet birds are prey animals, which means that they are accustomed to being hunted in the wild. Prey animals will often hide injuries and illnesses so that potential predators do not see them as vulnerable. A pet bird may be ill or hurting and show no outward signs of distress. As a result, it's important for pet bird owners to give their birds regular inspections and vet checkups.

EGG BINDING

Unlike chickens, who lay eggs whether or not they have been fertilized, female parrots generally do not lay eggs unless they have a mate. However, they may occasionally do so. The same is true of finches. Sometimes, the egg a female bird creates is underdeveloped, and it becomes stuck inside of her. The egg can also be stuck if the bird does not have strong enough muscles to push it out. This is known as egg binding. Egg binding can be fatal if the hen, or female bird, does not get help passing the egg. Veterinarians can help the hen pass a stuck egg by giving fluids or vitamin injections, or by simply helping to pull it out.

There are, however, ways that owners can monitor their pet's health. A healthy bird should have bright, clear eyes; clean nares (or nose holes); clean, shiny feathers; feet that grab well; and an alert attitude. Its beak and nails should not be overgrown. A parrot's beak and nails grow constantly, and the bird normally wears them down through chewing food and rubbing or perching on rough surfaces. But some birds don't wear down their beaks and nails enough on their own. These birds need their beaks and nails trimmed. Birds that seem depressed, have diarrhea, or undergo appetite changes are likely sick.

One common disease that affects pet birds is avian chlamydiosis, which birds can contract by breathing dust from infected birds' feathers or droppings. This bacterial disease can spread to humans, in whom it is known as parrot fever. Avian chlamydiosis can lead to death in both parrots and humans. Both birds and humans can also get avian tuberculosis, a bacterial disease that causes weight and muscle loss in birds.

Other common health problems include yeast infections, parasite infestations such as feather mites, and foot conditions such as bumblefoot, an infection usually related to poor nutrition. Regular checkups, good sanitary practices, quarantining of sick or new birds, and a good diet are some of the best defenses against these issues.

CHAPTER 4

PET BIRD WELL-BEING

Pet birds thrive when they feel safe and comfortable in their environments and when they receive high-quality, regular exercise. Birds also have curious, restless minds and need lots of time to learn, play, and explore. Pet owners can begin bonding with and entertaining their birds as soon as they come home. Whether a bird is a young fledgling or a fully grown adult, its owners should socialize it to help it feel happy and safe with its human companions.

SOCIALIZING BIRDS

Pet birds are naturally social animals. In the wild, they live in flocks and bond in pairs. Pet birds need to learn to channel their natural instincts into a human home environment. In addition, pet birds must learn to get used to human company,

Parrot chicks can learn to enjoy human interaction even while they are still being raised by their parents.

and ideally to being handled by people. The process of introducing birds to their humans and their fellow pets is called socialization.

It is easiest to socialize very young birds. Baby parrots and finches are altricial, which means that hatched birds are undeveloped and unable to feed themselves. In the wild, altricial birds are fed by their parents. However, some pet bird breeders choose to hand-feed baby birds after they are a few weeks old. In this way, some of the birds' first meals come from people. Since this form of socialization starts so early, it tends to make birds very comfortable with human company.

However, baby parrots also socialize with their parents and siblings in their first weeks, and overhandling by humans can interrupt that process. Regardless of whether a bird is hand-fed, younger birds are, in general, easier to bond with.

WEANING BIRDS

In the wild, baby birds are at first fed by their parents. Songbirds and parrots feed their young by regurgitating, or vomiting, food into their mouths. Pet birds are hand-fed by humans using methods that mimic this process. When baby birds start to lift objects with their beaks, they are ready to start weaning, or eating adult food. For a while, the bird's breeder or handler offers formula or baby food in addition to regular bird food. Eventually, the bird learns to eat on its own. Wild birds aren't fully weaned until they can fly on their own.

Pet owners should wait a few months, or until the bird is weaned, before taking the bird away from its parents and to its new home.

There is no need to pressure a bird into accepting human touch, but all pet birds should at least feel safe and secure being fed and looked at by people, as well as being handled for health care. Many finches are not interested in bonding with humans, although they may enjoy time with other birds. Socializing finches can involve talking to them in a soft, low voice, introducing them to new sounds, and touching their cages. If a finch is interested, owners can begin to finger train it, teaching the bird to use a finger as a perch.

Many parrots finger train easily. Treats are key to training. A number of bird species enjoy spray millet, and it can be used as an incentive. The first step is to get the

Like other animals, birds have a circadian rhythm, which is a natural cycle of behaviors and hormonal changes that occur alongside the day's 24-hour cycle. The light of the sun helps regulate birds' hormones and tells them when to sleep and wake up. Like humans, parrots also need vitamin D from sunlight. Since many pet birds come from tropical regions, they require a great deal of sunlight. Buying special ultraviolet light bulbs for indoor use, giving birds safe exposure to sunlight whenever possible, and covering the bird's cage at regular times all help regulate the bird's circadian rhythms.

bird comfortable with a human hand inside its cage. The pet owner can offer treats to get the bird to approach the hand and then slowly switch to a treat reward every time the bird steps up, or hops onto a finger. Over time, a bird that takes to finger training will step up whenever it wants to spend some time with its human friend.

Another key part of pet bird socialization is towel training. If a bird becomes sick or injured, it may need to go to the vet. Distressed, injured birds may avoid being handled or be unable to get themselves into a carrier. Towel training birds gets them used to being wrapped and carried inside a towel for safe transport. Bird trainers recommend first holding a towel and letting the bird jump and walk on it, reinforcing the behavior with treats. Then, the bird owner can progress to playfully wrapping the bird in a towel, making the experience a positive one. It's important that, should an emergency come, the bird isn't additionally stressed by being carried in a scary, unfamiliar way.

PLAYTIME FOR PET BIRDS

While different birds have different interests and routines, birds are typically active, curious animals who like to play and explore. In the wild, they spend their time flying, searching for food, getting to know new environments, and socializing with other birds. In captivity, birds need time to play with toys and interact with their environments. They should be able to play both inside and outside their cages.

Different birds have different playtime needs, but in general, parrots need a lot of stimulation. Their mental health can suffer greatly if they are bored or lonely. Each parrot should have a variety of different toys, more than can fit in the bird's cage at any given time. Then, the parrot owner can rotate out different toys with the bird's weekly cage deep cleaning. In this way, the bird is always receiving new toys to play with.

Parrots should also have supervised time outside their cages to walk or fly around and play with their human friends. Ideally, this playtime will happen as part of the bird's daily routine and be something it looks forward to. For example, pet cockatiels do best when played with and handled for about an hour a day, preferably around the same time daily. This playtime can be spent petting

Parrots should have a variety of toys to play with. They often love toys they can chew or shred and toys that make noises, such as bells or crinkle toys.

the bird, hanging out together, or learning new tricks. Other types of birds may require more or less time out of their cages playing and exercising.

TALKING, SINGING, AND TRICKS

Most birds don't need special training to begin mimicking certain sounds. In the wild, birds use their vocalizations to communicate with other members of their flock. Pet songbirds naturally vocalize and can learn and repeat new sounds.

Some pet parrots will also repeat words or phrases they hear frequently. Eventually, they can use these words to communicate with the humans they consider their flock. Parrot owners can channel their birds' talking abilities with rewards. Bird expert Nikki Moustaki says, "In the wild, parrots learn

OBSERVATIONAL LEARNING IN BIRDS

Observational learning is learning by watching. Many animals, humans included, learn how to accomplish basic tasks by watching their parents or the other animals around them. Pet birds are no exception. While some of their behaviors are innate, birds learn how to do many daily activities by observation. For example, birds learn from their companions which foods are and aren't safe to eat. Observational learning can be an important bird training tool, especially if a pet owner has multiple birds. For instance, a shy bird can watch a more outgoing bird get treats for performing a trick, and eventually the shy bird might decide that it would like to try training as well.

the language of the other parrots in the area. In a home, parrots learn the language of the home, which includes the voices of family members as well as household sounds."[1]

Moustaki explains that parrots want to communicate with the people around them, so they'll learn to imitate sounds that give them a response. Parrot trainers can harness this impulse by repeating and reinforcing with treats and praise the phrases they want to hear, like "good morning" and "I love you." It takes a while for most pet parrots to mimic human words clearly. Moustaki recommends rewarding when parrots clearly enunciate a desired word or phrase. Not all birds learn to talk. African grays and some Amazon parrots are among the most likely to learn words. But individuals in other species can learn too, and they enjoy the opportunity to apply their brains to the task.

With time and training, some birds can learn to perform an impressive array of tricks. For example, parrots can be taught to climb a ladder, slide down a slide, or push a ball. They can dunk a toy basketball in a hoop with their beaks. Some people may even be able to potty train their parrots, or teach them how to eliminate in one area of the cage only. Owners should make sure the birds are comfortable and not stressed during the training process. But for willing, curious birds, training time is valuable

AFRICAN GRAY

African grays are parrots native to a large part of Africa, from the western coast to as far east as Tanzania. Their name comes from their distinctive gray color, although they also have bright red tails.

They are about 12 to 16 inches (30–40 cm) long and weigh 8.8 to 23 ounces (250–650 g).[2] In the wild, these parrots eat a varied diet of mostly fruit supplemented with insects, clay, and other foods such as tree bark.

The Yoruba people of Nigeria incorporate the feathers of this parrot into one of their festivals. The birds' talkativeness and intelligence are recorded in Yoruba folklore. African grays are renowned for their intelligence and learning abilities. A 2019 study in the journal *Behaviour* found that African grays were better at some thinking tasks than the average five-year-old human. The study found that the birds could use logic and probability to figure out which of several cups would be most likely to contain a treat.

African grays are very social and bond closely with the people and birds around them. A 2020 study published in *Current Biology* found that these parrots sometimes help other parrots. Researchers trained African grays to give tokens to humans in exchange for nuts. Parrots would give some tokens to parrots with no tokens so they could also get nuts.

bonding with their humans as well as a source of exercise and stimulation.

FLIGHT AND EXERCISE

All pet birds need daily exercise to stay fit, healthy, and mentally well. Ideally, this includes regular flying time. Some birds have their wings clipped. The ends of their flying feathers are trimmed, making it very difficult for them to fly upward. Other birds are fully flighted, with untrimmed wings. Birds with clipped wings can exercise by walking around outside the cage, hopping from perch to perch or on furniture, and fluttering their wings so that they float to the ground.

Fully flighted birds can exercise by flying indoors in a bird-proofed home or in a home aviary. Other bird owners harness train their birds, taking them outside on a leash. Like finger training and towel training, teaching a bird to wear and fly on a harness requires special preparation. First, the bird must practice wearing the harness indoors until it is comfortable being harnessed. This may take a while, since some birds may find the look and feel of the harness scary at first. Once the bird is comfortable wearing a harness, owner and bird can progress to taking walks together. Bird owners should still be cautious, however. Properly attached harnesses can prevent a bird from flying away, but they will not necessarily protect a pet from predators such as hawks.

Some owners also practice free flying with their birds. Free flying involves letting a bird fly outside with no restrictions whatsoever. Birds who free fly must be trained to return to their human companions and must learn to become comfortable exploring new environments on their own. Free flying requires intensive training and comes with serious risks. There is no guarantee that a free flying bird will not fly away, become injured, or fall prey to a predator.

CHAPTER 5

THE PET BIRD INDUSTRY

Many pet bird owners start their bird ownership journey at the pet store. Pet store owners often act as go-betweens for bird breeders and would-be owners. A good pet store can also be the place where a pet bird owner gets the accessories and food that are necessary for a bird's health and well-being. Pet bird owners should make sure that the pet stores they visit are clean and well-maintained, and that the staff is knowledgeable about the birds the store sells. Good pet stores should be eager to provide information about their birds. They should be invested in their animals' health and well-being.

Not all bird owners get their birds and supplies from pet stores. Many pet supplies are now available online through sellers such as Chewy. Owners can also directly contact bird breeders instead of buying birds from pet stores. Good private breeders should also be eager

If buying from a store, people should try to find a store that specializes in birds or that has staff especially knowledgeable about birds if they have any questions.

to talk about the birds they sell, answer questions, and introduce buyers to available birds. Good breeders should have veterinary records for all their birds, should not breed their animals too often, and should make sure baby birds are fully weaned before they are sold.

People who do not want to buy birds from stores or breeders can search local shelters and rescues for adoptable birds. These organizations are typically nonprofits rather than businesses. However, they usually still charge adoption fees to cover their costs of operation, including veterinary care and food.

FOOD COMPANIES AND RECIPES

Many companies provide specialized pet food for birds. There are a few well-known bird food companies whose products can be found at mainstream pet stores. The Kaytee brand grew out of a seed company begun in the late 1800s. By the mid-1900s, the company started manufacturing wild bird seed. These were collections of seeds that people could use in outdoor bird feeders. Around this time, the company began selling feed mixes for pet birds such as budgies as well. Today, the Kaytee brand offers food for macaws, lovebirds, cockatiels, parakeets, canaries, other finches, and other pet birds. The brand includes daily food, treats, and food specially formulated for hand-feeding baby birds.

Pet stores sell bird products from a variety of companies. Owners should research which products and brands are the best fit for their birds.

Other pet food brands that make bird food include Vitakraft, Lafeber, and ZuPreem. These brands have certain attributes in common. They offer species-specific blends and bags of daily food as well as special treats.

The Food and Drug Administration (FDA) does not regulate pet food in the same way that it does food for people. Human food requires FDA approval before it can be sold. However, pet food companies are required to offer certain types of information to their customers.

In the United States, a package of bird food should offer a full ingredients list and a breakdown of the food's fat, protein, fiber, and moisture content. This breakdown must come in the form of percentages. For example, a bag of bird pellets could specify that its ingredients are 15 percent protein and 4 percent fat.[1]

Pet food manufacturers must also clarify which of their products are suitable for daily meals and which are treats or supplements. In addition, different states have their own pet food regulations. For example, the state of California requires pet food to be processed with a magnet that helps remove traces of metal.

Some companies offer special formulas for different stages of life, and some make foods for molting birds. Vitakraft, which makes and sells parakeet food, also makes an egg-based food that provides extra protein for stressed, anxious birds. While it may seem strange to give eggs to pet birds, the eggs can provide essential protein and fat. Egg food is commonly fed to breeding birds as well.

Some people make homemade bird food and sell it in person or through small-business websites such as Etsy. Homemade bird food makers may advertise that their products contain food that is higher quality than that found in commercial bird food. The seeds found in commercial bird food, for instance, often contain dyes and artificial coloring. Small-batch bird food sellers might advertise that their food is human quality. They may say it is made from ingredients found in grocery stores that are subject to FDA regulations.

However, pet bird owners should be wary of sellers who do not follow regulations for pet food packaging. Some bird experts recommend that pet bird owners create their own bird food blends. The bird care company BirdTricks, for example, offers recipe books and instructions for pet bird owners who wish to make their own bird food.

BIRD TOY AND CAGE COMPANIES

Some companies specialize in cages, toys, and accessories for birds. They sell cages and aviaries that are easy to set up. Companies that sell cages may also sell many cage accessories, such as mirrors, cage covers, bird swings, and cleaning supplies.

Pet companies also sell toys for birds. For example, Super Bird Creations is a Colorado-based company that was founded in 1992. The company organizes toys by purpose, such as stress relief or chewing fun. These categories allow bird owners to mix and match toys to provide for a variety of needs. Bonka Bird Toys is another pet company specializing in bird toys. One of the company's top sellers is the Sola Atta Ball, a ball made out of stems of the sola plant. Birds can push the ball, tear it apart, chew it, and explore it with their claws.

Pet bird owners who don't know which bird toys their pet might like best can also seek out bird-specific pet stores and retailers. The staff of these stores may be knowledgeable about the likes and dislikes of certain types of birds. For example, Bird Paradise in Burlington, New Jersey, boasts that it is the world's largest exotic bird store. Bird Paradise's staff are known as avian consultants, and the store hosts free educational events to teach customers about bird care and science. The store also offers ongoing education and resources to the customers who buy its birds.

RESOURCES AND STANDARDS

There are many resources available to pet bird owners who have questions about the right way to raise, train, or care for their pets. Some bird specialists and trainers sell books, videos, and courses that provide this information. For example, husband-and-wife pair Dave and Jamieleigh Womach began working with pet birds as part of a professional magic act. Eventually, the couple founded the company BirdTricks.

In addition to bird food and toys, the company offers a mix of paid and free training content. For example, BirdTricks posts free YouTube videos with tips on caring for a variety

BIRDS AND MIRRORS

Many pet birds enjoy looking at themselves in mirrors. Birds recognize that the animal they see in the mirror is a bird as well, and they can begin to befriend their own reflections. A lonely bird may appreciate the company of another bird companion when its humans cannot give it any attention. However, owners must take care that their bird does not become too fixated on the mirror. A bird who attacks a mirror or spends most of the day looking at it is not enriched by the mirror's presence.

of bird species. They also show how to train reluctant or shy birds. In addition, customers can pay for training courses on topics ranging from beginner bird care to free flying.

Besides online resources, there are also many books on pet birds. Bird enthusiasts can buy books on the basics of bird care as well as books that focus on one species in detail. The popular *For Dummies* series of books offers titles on bird, parrot, parakeet, and cockatiel care.

There are a few national and international organizations that offer general guidance on bird care. For example, the World Parrot Trust is a parrot advocacy organization. The group works to improve the welfare of both wild and pet parrots. The World Parrot Trust acknowledges that, in the past, people worldwide have raised birds without understanding or caring about their needs, and many parrots have suffered. However, it believes that keeping birds can be done well. "With the right knowledge and experience, many parrot keepers are able to share their lives with parrots in a manner which is mutually beneficial to parrots and people alike," it writes.[2]

The World Parrot Trust offers position statements, giving its official opinion on the best way to care for birds. For example, the World Parrot Trust is against the practice of clipping the wings of bircs, believing that flying is an essential part of a bird's nature. Other organizations offer basic information on several types of birds and basic standards for their care. The Animal Humane Society, for example, advocates for large cages for finches and reminds owners to provide their birds with regular veterinary care.

BIRD HEALTH CARE

Not all veterinarians are trained in pet bird care. While most cities and towns have at least one veterinarian, that person may not be ready to take on bird clients. Not all US veterinary schools teach avian medicine as part of their curricula. Becoming a certified avian veterinarian

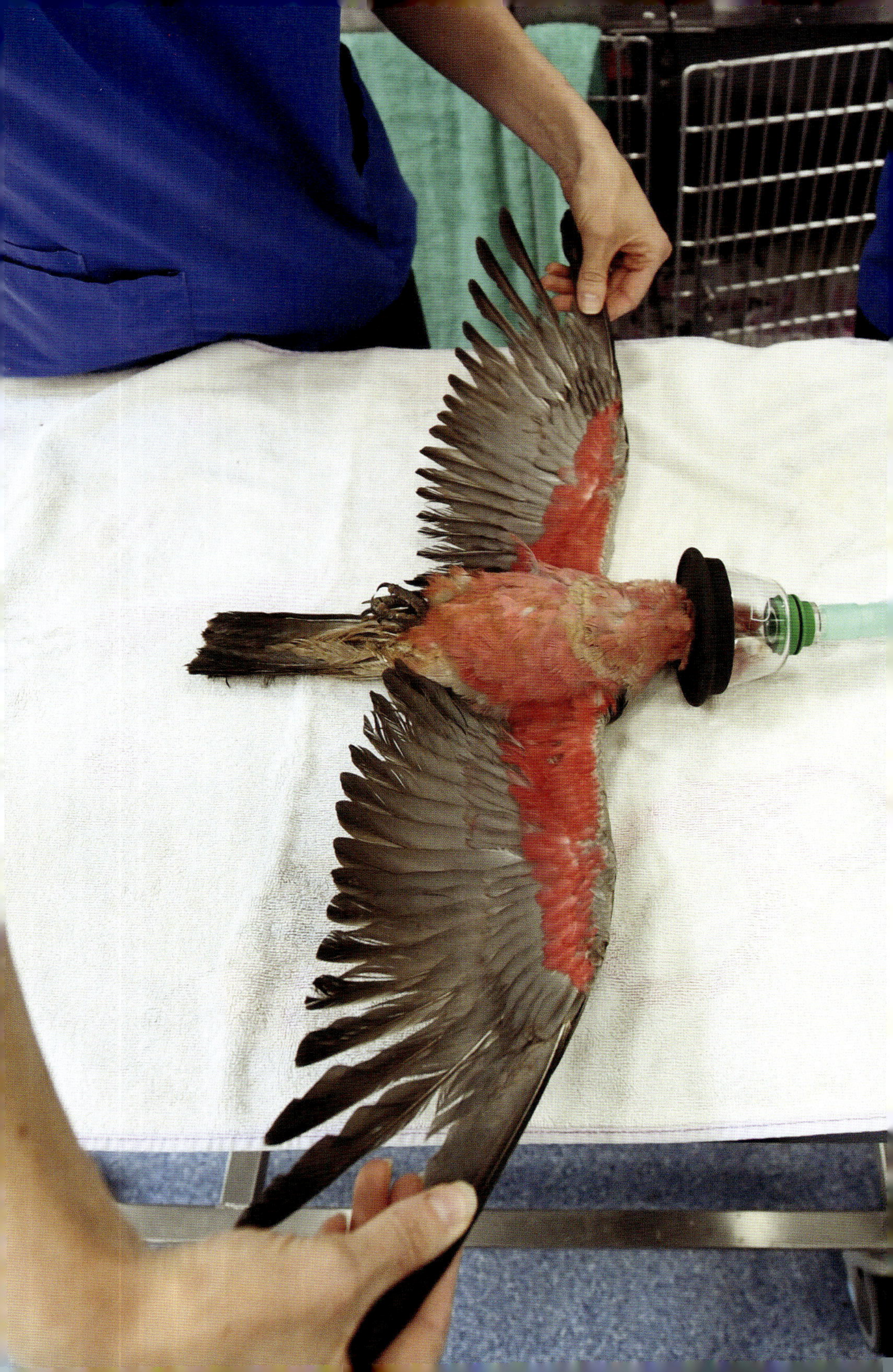

is a demanding path, involving years of extra training in addition to a veterinary degree's requirements.

Pet bird owners should locate a veterinarian with training in avian medicine. One good place to start looking for an avian veterinarian is the Association of Avian Veterinarians (AAV). The AAV has a directory of professionals trained in avian medicine organized by location. Bird owners can use this tool to find avian veterinarians in their area. The AAV also offers resources for pet bird owners. Its website features free pamphlets on the care of several different types of pet birds, as well as information on common bird illnesses. These informational pamphlets are available in nine languages.

Medical care for pet birds can be expensive, and pet bird owners should prepare themselves for the costs of checkups as well as emergencies. According to Wild Bird World, the average checkup visit for a pet bird costs about $30 to $100.[3] Overnight visits and special procedures for sick birds can cost hundreds or thousands of dollars.

CHAPTER 6

LAWS AND REGULATIONS

The legal landscape surrounding pet birds is complicated. There are business and environmental concerns regarding the bird trade and the health and safety regulations that pet stores and pet companies must follow. There are also concerns about animal welfare regulations for the ethical treatment of birds, as well as ownership concerns such as local noise ordinances that may affect chatty birds. Pet bird owners should make sure they follow national, state, and local laws on bird ownership. They should also be aware of the larger context of laws on the trade and treatment of pet birds.

THE PET BIRD TRADE

Since the early 1900s, it has been illegal to own most species of North American birds. As a result, the United States became one of many countries across

Wild birds captured in the illegal trade are often kept in cramped cages. Officials who find them release them back into the wild when possible.

the world looking to trade tropical birds. When air travel
became more commonplace after the 1950s, hundreds of
thousands of birds were caught and shipped from tropical
habitats to markets in Europe and the Americas. The wild
bird trade has a long history in Asia as well.

The capture, transport, and trade of millions of tropical
birds had a devastating effect on local habitats and animal
welfare. In 1967, Brazil responded to the massive loss of
wild bird populations by banning the sale of wild birds.
Many other countries eventually followed suit. In 1975, the
Convention on International Trade in Endangered Species
of Wild Fauna and Flora was written. The agreement
forbids trading animals in danger of extinction and has
been signed by 184 countries.[1]

In 1992, the United States passed the Wild Bird
Conservation Act, banning most wild exotic birds from
entering the country. Before the passage of the act,
the United States imported as many as 150,000 parrots
a year.[2] In 2022, a survey of 50 countries with native
parrot populations found that only two—Guyana and
Suriname—allowed the legal trade of birds caught in
the wild.[3]

Despite these laws and regulations, there is a thriving
illegal trade in wild birds. It is a business that operates
without any regulations for its workers or for the birds
they capture. Many wild-caught birds die or are injured

before they ever reach the market. The absence of health and safety regulations means that wild-caught birds are at a high risk of contracting and spreading diseases. While the wild bird trade is officially banned in the United States, illegally caught birds do make their way into the country and are put up for sale. Responsible pet owners have a duty to not support the illegal pet bird industry. It is vital to do thorough research on a pet store or breeder before purchasing a bird.

RESTRICTIONS ON PET BIRD OWNERSHIP

Pet birds tend to be noisy. They sing, talk, and vocalize in other ways, sometimes very loudly and for much of the day. Some birds are louder than others, but all pet bird owners should expect their bird to consistently make noise. They can also be messy and destructive pets. Because of the potential for persistent loud noise and damage, some apartment and housing complexes ban pet birds. It is legal for landlords to forbid birds from moving onto their property. Pet bird owners should be aware that they may not be able to move freely between homes with their bird in tow.

Some states also ban birds that may be permitted in other places. For example, the monk parakeet, also known as the Quaker parrot, is a species of parrot native to South America. It is known for building large nests out of sticks. Some pet monk parakeets have escaped or been released into wild areas of the United States and have

A monk parakeet nest can weight up to one short ton (0.9 metric ton).

begun reproducing. In some states, such as Texas and New York, their large nests damage power lines. It is illegal to own or sell a monk parakeet in some US states. Owners of monk parakeets should avoid moving to those states or bringing their parrots when traveling to those states.

Pet owners who have a male and female adult bird of the same species may wish to breed them and raise the offspring. While bird breeding is a natural process, there are state and local regulations on breeding and selling pet birds. These laws vary greatly by region and according to the type of bird. For example, in New York State, pet bird owners can breed some species, such as budgerigars and zebra finches, without a permit. A permit is required for exotic bird species not specifically listed by the law, however. In contrast, the state of Florida requires anyone who sells exotic birds, including breeders, to be licensed by the state.

RESTRICTED BIRD SPECIES

There are some birds that can be kept and raised under special circumstances. For example, North American owls cannot be bought and sold as pets inside the United States. However, it is possible to get a special permit to care for an injured or abandoned wild owl. Other raptors, such as eagles, hawks, and falcons, can also be kept with special permits. These birds are used to practice falconry, or bird-assisted hunting.

BIRDS IN INDONESIA

Indonesia is a country located on a series of islands between the continent of Australia and the southeast part of mainland Asia. Indonesia is home to many tropical forests and a population of more than 270 million people.[4] In addition, more than 1,700 species of birds live there.[5]

Indonesia is one of many countries worldwide that participates in the centuries-old tradition of songbird competitions. In these competitions, people train male songbirds to memorize complex melodies. Then the birds are placed near each other and evaluated by judges. There were more than 1,000 such competitions in Indonesia every year before the COVID-19 pandemic hit in 2020 and suspended the gatherings.[6]

Winning birds can be sold at high prices, and winning competitors can win thousands of dollars or prizes such as new cars.

Tangerang is one Indonesian city that holds songbird competitions.

Partly as a result of the demand for these birds, Indonesia's capital, Jakarta, is home to the largest market for birds in the region. However, the demand for songbirds comes at a steep environmental cost. Many of the birds sold in the songbird trade are caught in Indonesian forests, even though it is typically illegal to do so. Illegal capture and trade of birds has led to the Asian songbird crisis, which puts many Asian species at risk of extinction.

BIRD CUSTODY

Owning a pet bird can be a lifelong commitment. Some species of parrots can live more than 70 years.[7] In fact, the oldest known cockatoo, Cookie, was at least 82 when he died.[8] An adult who buys a long-lived parrot might be caring for a friend who will outlive them. Some people decide to prepare for this possibility by leaving provisions for their birds in their wills.

Legally, pets are considered personal property. If a person with a pet bird dies and does not mention the bird in the will, the animal will go to whomever receives the rest of the deceased's property. If a pet bird owner has someone specific in mind to care for their bird after their death, the owner can designate that person as the parrot's caregiver and leave money for the pet's upkeep. However, there is no guarantee that an assigned caregiver will take care of the bird well or spend money wisely.

Bird owners who want to be extra sure that their birds are taken care of can establish a trust for their birds. The trust gives money to an assigned bird caretaker. It also names someone called a trustee to make sure that the birds are being treated properly and the money for their needs is being spent appropriately.

Divorced couples who own a bird together can also seek legal solutions to manage the animal's custody and care. In divorce cases, birds are also considered property.

A judge can award a bird to one spouse or the other
but cannot insist on shared custody or an amicable
agreement. However,
some mediators will
work with divorcing
couples to figure out
who should get the pet
and whether shared
custody is possible.

LAWS ON ANIMAL TREATMENT

In the United States,
there are federal and
state laws that prohibit
cruelty against animals
and set standards for the
treatment of pets. These
laws are often complex and sometimes contradictory
because animals fulfill many different cultural and
environmental roles. For example, rats carry many
diseases that can spread to humans. Because of this, they
are considered pests in some contexts, and businesses
such as restaurants have a duty to try to exterminate
them. In a medical testing context, rats are laboratory

INTERNATIONAL TRAVEL WITH PET BIRDS

Traveling with a pet bird companion can be tricky. Many countries have strict regulations surrounding which animals they will allow inside their borders. The USDA's Animal and Plant Health Inspection Service provides information about the laws on bringing animals from one state or country to another. In addition, it is important to check that airlines will allow pet birds to travel. Some, but not all, airlines allow birds to travel in carriers under plane seats.

animals that must be kept under specific conditions. And to some people, rats are beloved pets.

US animal welfare laws tend to deal with animals according to their cultural roles. Birds are better known to most people as food animals or as wild animals than they are as pets. For example, Americans eat about eight billion chickens a year.[9] Meanwhile, only 7.5 million birds live as American pets.[10] Possibly for this reason, birds have traditionally been excluded from laws meant to set standards for animal treatment.

The United States' primary animal welfare law is the Animal Welfare Act, passed in 1966. This law regulates the treatment of commercially sold pets and zoo animals. However, the law originally offered no protections for birds. Bird treatment advocates challenged the US government to include captive birds in the law, and in 2002, the US government updated the definition of *animal* to include birds. However, it did not immediately write any standards for bird care, so the details of their protection remained unclear.

Even livestock laws that protect animals from being slaughtered in painful ways do not typically apply to birds such as chickens. In 2019, the US government passed the Preventing Animal Cruelty and Torture Act (PACT). This law made it illegal to torture small animals, including birds, for entertainment. Bird welfare advocates have continued to

push for more regulations ensuring the ethical treatment
of pet birds. In February 2022, the US Department of
Agriculture (USDA) announced that it would amend, or
change, the language of the Animal Welfare Act. The
department published standards of bird care for review.
The standards were scheduled to be finalized in 2023 and
would apply to captive birds not used for research.

BIRD DEBATES

While many pet bird owners fiercely love their animals, they can just as fiercely disagree about the best ways to care for their pets. Some of these debates are about making sure that pet birds have the best possible homes and living environments. A deeper question surrounds the issue of keeping essentially wild animals as pets. There are those who argue that the pet bird trade should stop entirely.

WING CLIPPING AND FLIGHT

It's common for pet birds to have clipped wings. When done correctly, the process is painless and reversible. A properly clipped bird has its wing feathers trimmed in a way that does not touch any of its blood vessels. And since birds molt and grow new feathers every few months, a clipped bird can always become an unclipped bird again.

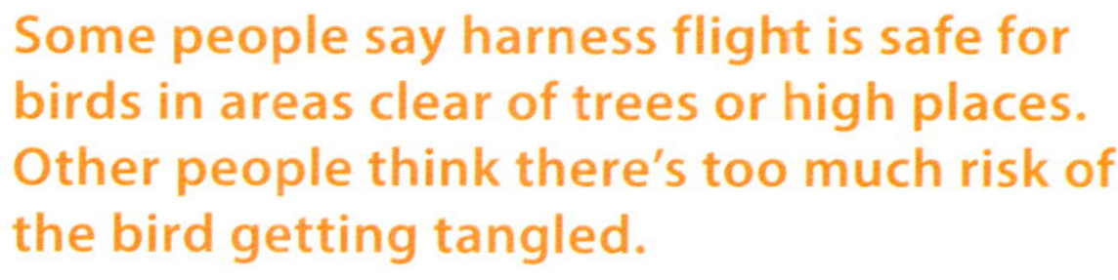

Some people say harness flight is safe for birds in areas clear of trees or high places. Other people think there's too much risk of the bird getting tangled.

Wing clipping involves cutting some, but not all, of the flight feathers.

However, some people argue that it is cruel to deprive a bird of its ability to fly. They point out that flying is the most natural form of exercise for a bird and that a bird's flying muscles make up a large and crucial percentage of its overall body. A clipped bird cannot reach the same level of physical fitness as a bird that flies regularly. Advocates for clipping point out that it can protect the bird from dangers inside the home and greatly reduce the likelihood that the bird will be able to escape into a dangerous environment. However, it is not a perfect solution. Birds with clipped wings can sometimes fly well enough to escape and get lost.

The AAV advises pet bird owners to consider clipping their bird's wings. It recommends that owners discuss the best course of action with an avian veterinarian. Meanwhile, the World Parrot Trust is against wing clipping, arguing that birds are happier and healthier when they can fly. Currently, the procedure is allowed in the United States, and avian veterinarians are trained to perform it safely.

Among bird owners who allow their birds to fly outside, there are disagreements about the relative safety of using a harness versus training a bird for free flight. Free flight trainer Hillary Hankey, for example, argues that putting birds on outdoor leashes increases their risk of injury. "The leash can easily get tangled in wings, branches, and any overhead objects, potentially ending in death for your bird if it hangs in a way that it cannot be freed," she says.[1] However, some of this risk can be avoided by flying birds away from trees.

Meanwhile, the parrot flight advocacy site Parrot Volancy argues in favor of both harnessed and free flight, depending on the bird and its surroundings. Free flight can be quite dangerous too. The bird might fly away and have to fend for itself in the wild, which captive-born animals are not usually equipped to do. It takes a lot of training to free fly a bird safely. And Parrot Volancy notes that larger birds tend to be better suited for free flight than smaller ones. They are less likely to be attacked by predator birds. Birds who cannot free fly safely can also fly indoors or in outdoor aviaries.

BREEDING

There are controversies around breeding birds too. Some breeders crossbreed different species or subspecies of parrots, creating hybrids that would not be found in the wild. Some parrot advocates advise against this, arguing that pet birds in captivity should be genetically similar to wild parrots. This is especially important, these people argue, because some wild parrot species are endangered. Having a purebred stock of tame birds could help some species survive.

Meanwhile, among domestic pet birds such as pigeons and chickens, it is both accepted and encouraged to breed animals that look nothing like their wild counterparts. Fancy pigeons, for example, are bred to have unusual characteristics, such as extra tail feathers, that average birds do not possess. Breeders achieve these animals by crossbreeding genetically similar birds over the course of generations. However, the selection for certain extreme features can also cause the birds to suffer from welfare problems. For example, the fantail pigeons bred for their striking tail feathers sometimes have trouble walking and

People around the world breed fancy pigeons such as fantails and compete in shows that judge which are the best examples of their types.

perching as a result of having excessive tail feathers that
are always flared.

Some people have also bred pigeons that occasionally
tumble in flight. While the tumbling usually lasts for only
a moment, and the bird usually continues flying on, it can
cause the birds to crash and become injured or even die.

The Universities Federation for Animal Welfare (UFAW),
an animal advocacy group in the United Kingdom, keeps
track of these types of welfare problems in pet animals.
The UFAW argues that several current breeds of fancy
pigeons are so disadvantaged that they should no longer
be bred. However, the UFAW also notes that there is a
lot still unknown about if and how different types of
abnormal feathers affect pigeon welfare, and the extent
of these effects also depends on how extreme the feature
is for the particular bird. Many fancy pigeon breeders
see their work as a kind of art form, elevating the beauty
of the birds through selective breeding. These pigeon
fanciers say that pigeon breeding is a hobby that can
teach people to care for animals and create lifelong bonds.

REHOMING AND BUYING BIRDS

Bird ownership itself has also come under scrutiny. It is
common for first-time bird owners to purchase a small,
cute, and inexpensive animal without having researched
how difficult it can be to care for. The rates of rehoming, or

finding new owners, for pet birds are very high. The Avian Welfare Coalition (AWC) is a US organization that counsels shelters and the public on exotic bird care. According to the AWC, thousands of pet birds every year are rehomed or surrendered to shelters. "Unfortunately, the traits that make parrots so intriguing are the same ones that

BONDING AND SEPARATION IN PET BIRDS

Parrots and finches are flock animals, and many species are known for their monogamous long-term partnerships. Pet birds who might have bonded with one bird in the wild can instead become very attached to a favorite person. They may be most drawn to the person in the house who understands their behavior best. There is a downside to these strong bonds, however. Birds can become very distressed if they feel abandoned by their caregivers and can act out by biting or ignoring a caregiver. Many parrot owners report postvacation aggression, which is when a parrot lets its caregiver know it feels abandoned by acting out.

make them extremely difficult to live with as companion animals," the AWC explains.[2] Many people are not prepared for the reality of living with a messy, loud, emotionally demanding, and sensitive animal.

When birds are surrendered or rehomed, their mental health is affected, and their behavioral problems can worsen. Stressed and lonely birds may bite, scream, act out sexually, or pluck out their feathers. The AWC, along with many other bird advocates, recommends that bird owners do a lot of research into the realities of life with their desired species. Bird owners should be prepared for an intensive, long-term commitment.

In addition, the AWC advocates that bird buyers find their birds at shelters and rescues rather than in stores.

The organization believes that captive bird breeding increases the demand for pet birds in general, indirectly supporting the wild bird trade. Not all bird lovers and bird welfare organizations agree with this stance. People may not be able to find the right bird for them in a rescue. Additionally, it can sometimes be easier to train a bird from a responsible breeder because it doesn't have as many established behavioral issues.

While some people debate the best source for a pet bird, others question whether these animals should be pets at all. Some bird owners may purchase and bond with a bird but later regret having a bird as a pet. They may come to feel guilty about not giving their animal the same freedom and stimulation it would enjoy in the wild. These owners may consider releasing the bird back into its natural habitat. It is possible to get the necessary permission

WILD BIRD RESCUES AND FOSTERS

In the United States, there are rescue centers and organizations that take in wild birds and rehabilitate them for release into the wild. For example, New York City's Wild Bird Fund treats and releases injured wild birds found in New York. Hundreds of species of native birds live in or pass through the city, where they are treated by the fund's staff. While the birds treated by the fund are not available for adoption, shelter volunteers can get hands-on experience caring for a variety of birds.

to travel internationally with a bird, and some bird release programs exist.

However, parrot experts and advocates strongly advise against releasing birds. The World Parrot trust explains that birds raised in captivity are not familiar with wild environments. Released birds are especially vulnerable to predators and may have trouble finding food and shelter. Instead of releasing captive birds, the trust recommends giving pet birds as much time and space to fly as possible.

For some people, loving pet birds means providing them with the happiest and healthiest lives possible. However, some bird and animal lovers think that parrots, finches, and other birds should never be kept as pets. Several animal rights organizations take this view. Animal welfare supporters advocate for making the lives of captive animals comfortable and providing for their physical and psychological needs whether they're pets, livestock, or laboratory research animals. In contrast, animal rights activists believe animals have the same rights as humans and often view captivity in any form, including as domestic pets, unethical, no matter how well the animal is cared for.

Animal rights supporters say that bird buyers can end up supporting the illegal bird trade and unethical bird breeders, whether they realize it or not. And it's common for pet birds to end up with owners who do

not know how to care for them properly or who become overwhelmed by the demands of bird ownership.

For these reasons, some animal rights supporters think no one should keep birds as pets. Some also say that birds should never be caged. However, animal rights supporters may recommend that people who wish to own pet birds should adopt from shelters only, rather than buying a baby bird at a store or from a breeder. Pet owners and animal welfare advocates say that many animals, including some species of birds, can thrive in captivity when given the care the particular species and individual needs.

CHAPTER 8

LIFE WITH PET BIRDS

In many ways, it is an exciting time to be a bird lover. Research into the emotional and mental capacity of birds has given people new insight into what these animals are truly capable of. And technology has made it easier for people to share what life with pet birds is really like. People who welcome birds into their lives often say that even though pet birds can be a lot of work, their animals play irreplaceable roles in their lives.

RESEARCH ON BIRDS

Birds have not always had a reputation for intelligence. The insult *birdbrain* for a silly person who lacks substance reflects a cultural belief that birds are simpleminded creatures. Research into the minds of many bird species, however, has shown that this is far from the truth. The more

For the right owners, a bird's intelligence and personality can make it an enjoyable pet.

people learn about the minds of birds, the more impressed they are by the inner workings of these animals.

In the 1970s, Dr. Irene Pepperberg graduated from Harvard University. Her PhD was in chemical physics, but she found herself most interested in studying an African gray parrot, Alex, that she had bought from a pet store. After some false starts, Pepperberg managed to get a grant to study Alex's ability to learn and think. Over the course of her bird's 31-year life, Pepperberg made some astonishing discoveries.

Alex learned more than 100 different words and phrases, which he could use in their appropriate contexts.[1] He could count to six. Alex could also identify objects by their color, shape, and material and could understand some basic mathematical concepts. By the end of his life,

Alex lived from 1976 to 2007.

he was working on learning to read by memorizing the sounds of different letters.

Before Pepperberg's research, scientists believed that only primates, the group of mammals that includes monkeys, apes, and humans, could understand and process language. They also believed that birds like Alex could only repeat sounds without understanding them. Pepperberg's research proved them wrong and led to an explosion of curiosity about the inner lives of birds.

As Pepperberg put it, "Birds are separated from humans by about 300 million years of evolution, give or take. Think about that: The last common ancestor was a dinosaur. And yet these birds are doing things that in some cases are equivalent to five- and six-year-old children."[2] Just because the brains

THEORY OF MIND IN BIRDS

Theory of mind refers to an animal's ability to imagine that other beings have thoughts and motivations that could be different from their own. It's sometimes called mentalizing. Humans tend to develop theory of mind very young, when they begin to understand that other people have their own separate thoughts and feelings. There is evidence that birds are also capable of mentalizing. For example, a 2016 study in *Nature Communications* found evidence that ravens worried about being spied on. This means they can imagine that other birds may want to watch them and observe what they do.

of birds are very different from those of humans does not mean they are not fascinating and complex in their own right.

More recent research has built on Pepperberg's insights, providing more information on the minds and capabilities of parrots and other pet birds. A 2022 study by members of the Max Planck Institute of Animal Behavior found evidence that parrots' long life spans may be linked to their intelligence. The study speculated that more intelligent birds might be better equipped to meet life's challenges, learning strategies that help them escape danger.

The researchers also suggested that, like humans, intelligent parrots might benefit from a childhood of learning from parents and older relatives. This long period of development could give the birds a variety of skills in adulthood. The researchers found evidence to support both hypotheses. The researchers wanted to continue to study the early lives of parrots and compare them to human childhood development.

Other research into pet birds has explored their complex social worlds. For example, another 2022 study from the Max Planck Institute found that male zebra finch songs have different dialects that help identify the finch's origin and social group. Female finches partly base their choice of mate on the dialect the male finch sings.

CONNECTING WITH OTHERS

The lives of bird owners are enriched because of their pets. Pet bird owners who immerse themselves in the world of the bird fancy can find many other people who share their interest in these fascinating animals. There are competitions, conventions, and volunteer events where bird lovers can meet each other. For example, cities across the United States frequently host exotic bird expos, or expositions. At these events, people can meet bird supply sellers and look at or buy exotic birds. These expos can be a good way to connect with other pet bird owners. There is at least one national exotic bird competition: the annual National Bird Show in Tulsa, Oklahoma. At this event, parrot owners compete to see who has the most beautiful and appealing bird.

Bird owners can also connect on websites such as Reddit, posting

EXOTICSCON

ExoticsCon is a yearly convention for members of the exotic pet industry. *Exotic animals* is a catchall term for nontraditional pets such as birds, reptiles, and tropical fish. The convention is typically held in a US city, although a virtual convention occurred during the COVID-19 pandemic. At the convention, exotic veterinarians can meet and share information with companies that provide medical equipment and pet care. Professionals can share new ways to treat exotic pets. For example, the 2021 convention had a workshop on exotic animal hematology, or blood analysis.

BIRD SOCIAL MEDIA STARS

Some birds have found fame on social media, where their tricks and lovable antics have gained them an audience. For example, TikTok user blubelle.the.bird has more than 60,000 followers.[3] The owner of the account posts videos of their blue budgie Blubelle chatting, hanging out, and showcasing his lively personality. Bird owners and people who don't have birds follow along with Blubelle's antics. The user also shares details of their experience bonding with Blubelle, explaining, for example, that he used to bite them but no longer does.

photos, videos, and stories, showing off their pets, and giving a window into what life is like with a bird companion. For example, users may post a series of photos of their birds caring for new chicks. Users may also ask for advice, such as how to avoid egg binding in canaries, and other bird owners can give tips. Conversations like this also take place on other online forums and on social media pages and groups.

Some bird lovers may not have the time or the space to welcome their own bird. These people can volunteer to work with abandoned birds at animal shelters. For example, Best Friends Animal Sanctuary's Parrot Garden in Kanab, Utah, welcomes volunteers who want to play and socialize with birds waiting for homes. They can connect with other bird lovers and learn about bird care.

Birds can help their owners connect with other humans in unexpected ways too. Brooklyn, New York, barbershop owner Fausto Stilo has a pet rooster named

Dulce de Leche who keeps him company during the day. Many people, from the kids in the elementary school across the street to his customers, come by to say hello and bond with the bird. Stilo lives in a diverse neighborhood, with immigrants from many different countries, and many of them say that seeing a chicken reminds them of home. "When they tell me that, it's like I'm making their day," Stilo told the *New York Times*.[4]

THE JOYS OF PET BIRDS

Pet bird owners' experiences are as diverse as the animals they take care of. But despite the differences in their individual bird friends, many human companions report finding daily joy in the liveliness, intelligence, beauty, and affection of their animals. They talk about birds' capacities to learn and surprise.

Amanda lives in Canada with her husband and children on a piece of land they call the Useless Farm. The animals Amanda and her family keep include several peacocks and a pair of emus. Amanda jokes that one of the emus, Karen, considers herself Amanda's enemy. Amanda posts videos on TikTok of Karen the emu trying to attack her. Amanda must forcefully raise her hand to prevent Karen's assaults. Despite Karen's feisty personality, Amanda loves her life with her unusual pets. "All of these animals bring me so much joy," she explained to a reporter.[5] "Karen is my soul sister," Amanda said in another interview, pointing out that she respects her bird friend's independence.[6] The daily excitement her bird frenemy provides is worth the occasional bruise or scrape.

Other pet bird owners echo Amanda's feelings. Birds can be noisy, messy, high-maintenance, and beaky—or nippy—but they are also colorful, interesting, and joyful. Emu owner Alexandra Douglas also fell under the spell of emu ownership, finding herself wanting to get as many of the birds as she could support on her land. "It all started with one," Douglas wrote for a poultry blog, "and then I had to get more."[7]

Other bird owners also find themselves drawn to the independence and uniqueness of their bird companions. Parrot owner Sarah acknowledges that her birds are not as easy to tame and eager to please as more domesticated pets might be. But she believes that makes life with her birds more interesting. "Parrots are true to who they are," Sarah writes. "[Each] one of them is unique."[8]

Pet finch owners find that their songbirds liven up their days with the noises they make. Editor Bria Sandford bought a canary in 2020, when she was living alone. "He has brought only delight," she wrote in an article, "despite sounding like a small car alarm when he's excited."[9] Sandford also wrote that her new pet helped her start new conversations about birds; some of her work

EMU

The emu is a land bird native to Australia. It is the second-largest bird in the world after the ostrich. Emus can grow to more than five feet (1.5 m) tall. They are covered in brown-gray feathers and have long, curved necks. Emus are powerful runners, reaching up to 30 miles per hour (50 kmh).[10]

Although they have wings, emus are unable to fly. They eat insects and fruit and live in flocks. There used to be many flightless bird species in Australia, and a species of emu was native to the island of Tasmania. However, many flightless birds on the continent went extinct due to human hunting.

Emus are used as sources of eggs, meat, oil, and leather. They can also make interesting and unusual pets. However, emus need a great deal of outdoor space to thrive. They require fences taller than they are, an outdoor space of at least 1,000 square feet (93 sq m), an outdoor shelter, and about 1.5 pounds (0.7 kg) of food a day.[11]

Experts recommend that pet emu owners purchase their birds young so that the birds grow up to be comfortable around their human companions.

colleagues would hear her canary sing and suggest that she work on books about birds.

For young bird owners, taking care of a pet bird for the first time can be a tough but exciting responsibility. It can also present new opportunities and challenges. Elle is a young content creator who discovered her love of birds when she was a toddler. By the time she was a teenager, Elle had her own flock of six parrots. In 2018, she began posting YouTube videos, talking about life with her birds and giving advice to other young people who wanted to become pet owners. Eventually, Elle began selling her own bird toy kits and advertising other products on her channel.

Elle says that her passion is "improving the lives of pet birds."[12] Although Elle loves her birds, she is realistic about the challenges of bird ownership. "They're basically like inviting a flying toddler into your house," she says in one video. Ultimately, though, Elle appreciates that her love of her birds has brought her daily companionship, fun, and an interesting career. "I would never change a thing," Elle says about her busy life balancing high school and the care of multiple pets. "Birds are just so amazing."[13]

Many pet birds are very social. It's important to spend a lot of time with them daily by giving them special attention and including them in daily routines.

ESSENTIAL FACTS

OWNING A BIRD

Birds are social, intelligent pets who need a great deal of daily care.

DIET: Most pet birds eat a mixture of fruits, vegetables, nutritional pellets, and seeds. Many pet birds can also eat insects or eggs for protein.

SPACE: Birds should be kept in cages that are at a minimum wide enough to allow for stretching their wings and climbing. They should also have space for toys, perches, food, and water, but the bigger the cage, the better.

ROUTINE CARE: Birds require fresh water at all times. Their cages should be cleaned daily, and they should have regular opportunities to bathe in water.

ENRICHMENT: Birds are inquisitive and need a variety of toys as well as regular time outside their cages. Many birds enjoy flying indoors, in outdoor aviaries, or outdoors.

KEY SPECIES

- The African gray parrot is renowned for its intelligence and learning abilities.
- Budgerigars, also called budgies or parakeets, are small, chatty parrots native to Australia.
- Cockatiels are small, crested parrots known for their friendliness.
- Emus are large, flightless birds sometimes farmed for their meat. They can also be kept as pets.
- Colorful singing canaries are the most popular finch species kept as pets.
- Some people breed and show fancy pigeons, selected for their unusual characteristics.
- Macaws are a large, intelligent, and colorful group of parrot species.

avian
Having to do with birds.

bacterial
Having to do with bacteria, which are microscopic living things that sometimes cause disease.

dialect
A regional variety of a language with distinct vocabulary, grammar, and accent.

domestic
Adapted to live among or be of use to people.

finger training
Teaching a bird to step onto a human finger.

fledgling
A young bird that has gotten its flight feathers.

flock
A social group of birds.

free flying
Allowing pet birds to fly outside without harnesses.

genetically
Relating to genes, which control the traits of a living thing.

hen
An adult female bird.

innate
A quality or ability one is born with.

metabolism
The physical and chemical means by which an organism processes energy.

molt
To shed feathers before growing new ones.

monogamous
Having only one mate at one time.

plume
A large, showy feather or group of showy feathers.

rehabilitate
To help recover from an injury or illness.

repertoire
The body of music one is capable of performing.

stimulation
Something that excites activity of the mind or body.

towel training
Teaching a bird to tolerate being wrapped in a towel.

wean
To switch baby birds from parental feeding to self-feeding.

SELECTED BIBLIOGRAPHY

Davids, Angela. *Cockatiels: A Guide to Caring for Your Cockatiel.* BowTie, 2006.

Hankey, Hillary. "So You Want to Train Your Pet Parrot for Free Flight." *Avian Behavior International*, 5 July 2022, avian-behavior.org. Accessed 14 Sept. 2022.

Moustaki, Nikki. *Parrots for Dummies.* John Wiley and Sons, 2021.

FURTHER READINGS

Hand, Carol. *The Evolution of Birds.* Abdo, 2019.

Moustaki, Nikki. *Parakeets for Dummies.* John Wiley and Sons, 2021.

Ringstad, Arnold. *Essential Birds.* Abdo, 2022.

ONLINE RESOURCES

To learn more about pet birds, please visit **abdobooklinks.com** or scan this QR code. These links are routinely monitored and updated to provide the most current information available.

MORE INFORMATION

For more information on this subject, contact or visit the
following organizations:

Association of Avian Veterinarians (AAV)

PO Box 9
Teaneck, NJ 07666
office@aav.org
aav.org

The Association of Avian Veterinarians (AAV) is an international
organization that works to promote bird health, welfare, and
conservation. Its members include many experts in bird health,
and its website provides resources for pet bird owners.

Avian Welfare Coalition (AWC)

PO Box 40212
St. Paul, MN 55104
info@avianwelfare.org
avianwelfare.org

The Avian Welfare Coalition (AWC) works to promote the
ethical care of captive birds. It offers educational outreach
programs as well as online resources to teach potential bird
owners how to ethically care for their animals.

World Parrot Trust

PO Box 985
Travelers Rest, SC 29690
parrots.org

The World Parrot Trust is a global organization that works
to educate people about both wild parrot conservation and
captive parrot care. It also offers recommendations for pet bird
owners on various issues such as wing clipping.

SOURCE NOTES

CHAPTER 1. FRIDAY FLYDAY

1. Nikki Moustaki. *Parakeets for Dummies.* John Wiley and Sons, 2021. 2.

2. Samantha Harris. "How Much Should a Healthy Budgie Weigh?" *Budgie Central*, n.d., budgiecentral.com. Accessed 17 Feb. 2023.

3. "Budgerigars." *Bush Heritage Australia*, n.d., bushheritage.org.au. Accessed 5 Jan. 2023.

4. "Birds Kept as Pets." *Centers for Disease Control and Prevention*, 28 Oct. 2019, cdc.gov. Accessed 24 Jan. 2023.

CHAPTER 2. THE HISTORY OF PET BIRDS

1. Hannah Ritchie, Fiona Spooner, and Max Roser. "Biodiversity." *Our World in Data*, 2022, ourworldindata.org. Accessed 5 Jan. 2023.

2. "US Pet Ownership Statistics." *American Veterinary Medical Association*, n.d., avma.org. Accessed 5 Jan. 2023.

3. Frank Gill and Glen E. Woolfenden. "Psittaciform." *Encyclopedia Britannica*, 9 Mar. 2018, britannica.com. Accessed 5 Jan. 2023.

4. "Psittaciformes—Parrots, Parakeets, Macaws, Cockatoos." *Wildlife Journal Junior*, n.d., nhpbs.org. Accessed 5 Jan. 2023.

5. Melissa Murray. "Zebra Finch." *Australian Museum*, 12 Dec. 2020, australian.museum. Accessed 5 Jan. 2023.

6. Marina Somma. "How Do I Know When My Zebra Finch Bird Is Pregnant?" *Sciencing*, 30 Sept. 2021, sciencing.com. Accessed 5 Jan. 2023.

7. A. R. Fishbein, S. L. Lawson, R. J. Dooling, and G. F. Ball. "How Canaries Listen to Their Song: Species-Specific Shape of Auditory Perception." *Journal of the Acoustical Society of America*, vol. 145, no. 1, Jan. 2019, ncbi.nlm.nih.gov. Accessed 5 Jan. 2023.

CHAPTER 3. PET BIRD CARE

1. Nikki Moustaki. *Parrots for Dummies.* John Wiley and Sons, 2021. 369.

2. Scot McDonald and Karrie Noterman. "Wingspan/Cage Measurements." *Parrot Education, Adoption, and Rehoming League*, Jan. 2016, pearlparrots.com. Accessed 5 Jan. 2023.

3. "What Size Enclosure Does My Pet Bird Need?" *RSPCA*, 8 Dec. 2021, kb.rspca.org.au. Accessed 5 Jan. 2023.

4. "What Size Enclosure?"

CHAPTER 4. PET BIRD WELL-BEING

1. Nikki Moustaki. *Parrots for Dummies*. John Wiley and Sons, 2021. 863.

2. Richard Pallardy. "African Gray Parrot." *Encyclopedia Britannica*, 28 May 2020, britannica.com. Accessed 5 Jan. 2023.

CHAPTER 5. THE PET BIRD INDUSTRY

1. "Lafeber's Tropical Fruit Pellets Cockatiel Dry Food, 25 Lbs." *Petco*, n.d., petco.com. Accessed 5 Jan. 2023.

2. "Position: Keeping and Breeding Parrots." *World Parrot Trust*, n.d., parrots.org. Accessed 5 Jan. 2023.

3. "How Much Does a Pet Bird Cost?" *Wild Bird World*, n.d., wildbirdworld.com. Accessed 5 Jan. 2023.

CHAPTER 6. LAWS AND REGULATIONS

1. "What Is CITES?" *Convention on International Trade in Endangered Species of Wild Fauna and Flora*, n.d., cites.org. Accessed 5 Jan. 2023.

2. "Critical Analysis: The Effectiveness of Current Laws Regulating the International Exotic Bird Pet Trade." *Denver Journal of International Law & Policy*, 24 Mar. 2014, djilp.org. Accessed 5 Jan. 2023.

3. P. Romero-Vidal, M. Carrete, F. Hiraldo, G. Blanco, and J. L. Tella. "Confounding Rules Can Hinder Conservation: Disparities in Law Regulation on Domestic and International Parrot Trade within and among Neotropical Countries." *Animals (Basel)*, vol. 12, no. 10, May 2022, ncbi.nlm.nih.gov. Accessed 5 Jan. 2023.

4. "Population, Total—Indonesia." *The World Bank*, n.d., data.worldbank.org. Accessed 5 Jan. 2023.

5. "Indonesia." *Bird Life International*, n.d., datazone.birdlife.org. Accessed 5 Jan. 2023.

6. Richard C. Paddock. "Bought for a Song: An Indonesian Craze Puts Wild Birds at Risk." *New York Times*, 18 Apr. 2020, nytimes.com. Accessed 5 Jan. 2023.

7. "How Long Do Parrots Live as Pets?" *Fetch by WebMD*, 8 July 2021, pets.webmd.com. Accessed 5 Jan. 2023.

8. "Oldest Parrot Ever." *Guinness World Records*, n.d., guinnessworldrecords.com. Accessed 5 Jan. 2023.

9. Kelsey Piper. "How Chickens Took Over America's Dinner Plates, in One Chart." *Vox*, 19 Feb. 2021, vox.com. Accessed 5 Jan. 2023.

10. "US Pet Ownership Statistics." *American Veterinary Medical Association*, n.d., avma.org. Accessed 5 Jan. 2023.

CHAPTER 7. BIRD DEBATES

1. Hillary Hankey. "So You Want to Train Your Pet Parrot for Free Flight." *Animal Behavior International*, 5 July 2022, avian-behavior.org. Accessed 5 Jan. 2023.

2. "Keeping Parrots as 'Pets.'" *The Avian Welfare Coalition*, n.d., avianwelfare.org. Accessed 5 Jan. 2023.

CHAPTER 8. LIFE WITH PET BIRDS

1. "Alex 1976–2007." *The Alex Foundation*, n.d., alexfoundation.org. Accessed 5 Jan. 2023.

2. Rebecca Boyle. "How Irene Pepperberg Revolutionized Our Understanding of Bird Intelligence." *Audubon*, 27 Mar. 2018, audubon.org. Accessed 5 Jan. 2023.

3. "bluebell.the.bird." *TikTok*, n.d., tiktok.com. Accessed 5 Jan. 2023.

4. Alexandra Genova. "You've Seen a Bodega Cat. How About a Barber Shop Rooster?" *New York Times*, 3 Sept. 2022, nytimes.com. Accessed 5 Jan. 2023.

5. Brooke Houghton. "An Ontario TikToker Runs a 'Useless Farm' with Her Family & Has a Dramatic Emu Named Karen." *Narcity Toronto*, 25 Apr. 2022, narcity.com. Accessed 5 Jan. 2023.

6. Eglė Radžiūtė. "Millions of People Can't Get Enough of the 'Useless Farm's' Animals, Especially an Emu Named Karen, Who's out for Blood." *BoredPanda*, 2022, boredpanda.com. Accessed 5 Jan. 2023.

7. Alexandra Douglas. "My Experience Raising Emus (They Make Great Pets!)." *Backyard Poultry*, 1 Feb. 2022, backyardpoultry.iamcountryside.com. Accessed 5 Jan. 2023.

8. "Why I Love Parrots as Companion Animals." *Three Birds and a Cloud*, 4 July 2014, threebirdsandacloud.wordpress.com. Accessed 5 Jan. 2023.

9. Bria Sandford. "After a Week or Two in New Hampshire, I Worry That I'm Regressing as an Adult." *Spectator*, 27 Mar. 2021, thespectator.com. Accessed 5 Jan. 2023.

10. "Emu." *Encyclopedia Britannica*, 1 Sept. 2022, britannica.com. Accessed 5 Jan. 2023.

11. Kathryn Copeland. "Do Emus Make Good Pets? What You Need to Know!" *PetKeen*, 27 July 2022, petkeen.com. Accessed 5 Jan. 2023.

12. "About: Meet Elle." *Elle and the Birds*, n.d., elleandthebirds.com. Accessed 5 Jan. 2023.

13. "The Reality of Living with Parrots When You're in School! *Should Kids Own Birds?*" *YouTube*, uploaded by ElleAndTheBirds, 27 Apr. 2020, youtube.com. Accessed 5 Jan. 2023.

INDEX

A. W. Buckey is a writer living in Brooklyn, New York. She shares a nickname with Alex the gray parrot.